For Jane McKenna
Very Best Wishes
and
Magic Dreams

Alexandra Kurland
and
Kenyon Bear

SHUTTLE HILL HERB SHOP
DELMAR, NEW YORK

TEDDIES
TO THE RESCUE

A KENYON BEAR BOOK

written by
Alexandra Kurland

with drawings by
Mark Kenyon

Bear Hollow Press

Delmar   New York

For Peregrine Meneldor
in whose year this was made

Requests for permission to make copies of any part of the work

should be mailed to:

Permissions, Bear Hollow Press

110 Salisbury Road

Delmar, New York 12054

Printed in the United States of America

Library of Congress Cataloging in Publication Data

Kurland, Alexandra. Teddies to the Rescue.

(A Kenyon Bear book)

Summary:Kenyon Bear and the other teddy bears in his shop

form a rescue party when they learn that one of their number

is being mistreated by his new owner.

[1. Teddy bears – fiction] I. Kenyon, Mark, ill.

II. Title. III. Series: Kurland, Alexandra. Kenyon Bear book.

PZ7.K958Te 1986   [Fic]   86-17389

ISBN 0-938209-27-2   ISBN 0-938209-22-1 pbk.

Table Of Contents

INTRODUCTION

I'd like you to meet my friend Kenyon Bear. He lives in the window of our local herb shop, and . . .

What's that – I didn't quite hear you. Oh! – What's a Herb Shop!

Well, it's . . . , it's ah – well, it's hard to explain. It's something like a gift shop, only not really. It's jammed crammed from floor to ceiling with flowers and wreaths and sweet smelling soaps. I suppose that's why grown-ups like it. But I like it for the bears. they live in the front window, and they're all made by hand by a very special lady. I think that's what makes them so magic.

Kenyon is the shop's bear. He lives in the window all year round. At Christmas he dresses up as Santa Bear and hands out gifts to all the other bears.

At Easter he puts on long rabbit ears and pretends he's the Easter Bunny.

In between times he dresses to suit the season, and the other bears join him. They're so funny. In the summer they go swimming with inner tubes and flippers. At Halloween they dress up in scary ghost costumes and go Trick or Treating.

And sometimes, just sometimes, Kenyon steps out of the window. He puts on his best hat, straightens the ribbon around his neck, and comes to tea with me. We sit for hours and hours, and he tells me wonderful stories. Some of them are very sad. (It's hard to believe, but not all teddy bears are loved.) Some of them are funny. They make me laugh and laugh until my sides ache. Some of them, I think he makes up, but most of them are real.

Shall I tell you one of his stories? Which one would you like to hear? How about . . . , I know, how about *Teddies To The Rescue*. It's a great story. Let's see, how does it begin . . . .

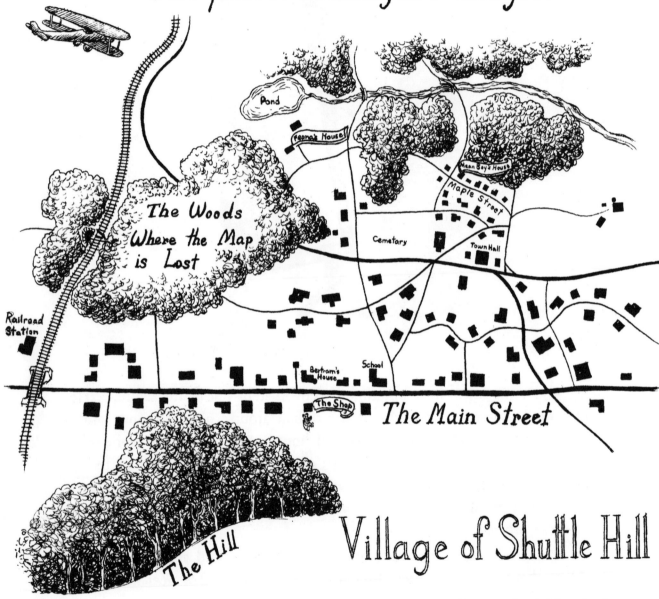

The places in Kenyon's story...

Pond

Feona's House

Mean Boy's House

Maple Street

The Woods
Where the Map
is Lost

Cemetary

Town Hall

Railroad
Station

Bertram's
House

School

The Shop

The Main Street

The Hill

Village of Shuttle Hill

As Charted by
Bertram B.

CHAPTER ONE
Amber Sends For Help

My friend, Kenyon Bear, is a very tidy bear. He hates a mess. Every night when the shop is closed and the traffic in the street has slowed to a trickle, he steps down out of the window. He and the other bears clean the shop from top to bottom. Kenyon vacuums and straightens all the high hard to reach places. The cubby bears dust, and the bigger bears restock all the shelves.

And when their chores are done, they play. They play teddy bear games. They play *hide-and-go-seek*, and *red light-green light*. They play *statues* (bears are very good at statues), and *Simon Says*, and *pin the tail on the donkey*.

But in the morning they are all back in their places. They smile their broad teddy bear smiles, and wave at the world rushing past. At nine o'clock every morning the mailman drops the mail through a slot in the door.

All the letters and magazines make an untidy jumble on the floor. Kenyon hates to see it. When the street is quiet again, he steps out of the window and gathers them all into a pile. He sets them up on the shop owner's desk. But first he looks through the letters.

Every now and then one of the bears who has been adopted will write him a note. He loves hearing from his old friends. They tell him wonderful stories about their new families. Kenyon sighs. He is everybody's favorite bear. They wave to him as they walk past and come to visit him in the shop. That delights him. But sometimes he wishes he could be somebody's own very special bear.

On this particular morning Kenyon saw a letter addressed to him. It was written in a very clumsy paw.

Kenyon groaned. He remembered Amber. He was a pretty honey colored bear. He had been so excited when he was adopted, especially when he learned that he was to be a present for a little boy.

"Just like Winnie the Pooh and Christopher Robin," he had giggled.

Indeed, yes, thought Kenyon. Amber was a sweet bear, but he had never been very clever.

He opened the letter and began to read. It was difficult going because the writing was so wobbly. Kenyon read slowly, but after the first sentence his smile left him. By the third he was growling under his breath. By the sixth he let out a loud grr-growl and brought his fist down **bang** on the window ledge.

"What is it? What's wrong?" cried all the other bears.

"This isn't right!" Kenyon exclaimed. "Here, listen to this," He read the letter out to his friends.

Dear Kenyon,

I really hate to write, but i dont know whatelze to do. I am so unhappy. The little boy who owns me is so mean. Hes pulled off my ear and poked holes in my stuffing. He even dropped me in the bathtub. I thought i was going to drown. I would run away if I could, but there iz a big Dog in the yard. I'm scared it would tear me to piecez. I dont know what you can do, but i need your help. Pleaze think of something.

Hurry, Amber

Kenyon finished reading the letter. "We've got to do *something*." he declared. And all the other bears agreed.

The younger ones wanted to rush off right there and then to rescue Amber, but Kenyon stopped them.

"We can't go off with so many people about, not during the day. We must have a plan. We must think."

He tucked the letter away where no one would see it and went back to his place in the window. A few minutes later the shop opened and a steady stream of people came in through the door. But that day none of the bears were smiling. They made ugly faces and tried to look fierce so no one would adopt them. And indeed nobody did.

CHAPTER TWO
The Car

At five-thirty the lights went out, and the doors were locked. Kenyon waited for it to get quiet outside, then he stepped down out of the window and went straight into the back storage room. He fished about until he found what he was looking for, a map of Shuttle Hill. He had seen the shop's owner using it just that afternoon to give directions to a customer.

He brought it out and spread it out on the floor by the window. Then he brought out the envelope with the return address written on it.

Maphe St., Maphe – what a funny name. But no, it wasn't Maphe, it was Maple, Maple Street.

The other bears gathered round him. They searched the map trying to find Maple Street.

"There it is, there it is!" cried a little brown bear. He jumped up and down in his excitement, and almost lost track of his place.

"But that's miles away," said another bear. "We can't possibly walk all that way."

And indeed, it did look a long, long way away on the map.

"We certainly can't all go," said Kenyon, "not walking. But two of us could go in the car. Though what two bears can do against a dog, I'm sure I don't know."

"Well, we have to try," said Christopher Bear. He was a gold bear with a wise old face, and all the other bears respected him. "We just have to hope we think of something once we get there. That's the best way to make any plan."

Now you may be wondering how teddy bears can go anywhere by car. Well, the answer is very simple because sitting in the middle of the window was a big green touring car.

The bears loved to play in it. They took turns sitting behind its steering wheel. They liked to pretend they were going for long drives in the country. And now two of them really would be going for a real ride on real roads. It wasn't pretend anymore.

Kenyon wished he could go, but he was too big to fit in the car. So he chose Christopher to drive it, and another bear named Pippin to go along to help.

They waited until well after dark to start out. When the road was quiet, Kenyon unbolted the front door. With a great deal of panting and grunting, and heave ho-ing, he jerked it open.

"Hooray! Hooray!" cheered all the shop bears, and "Good-luck," and "Be Careful."

Christopher and Pippin waved good-bye. The car sputtered out through the front door. It bounced across the sidewalk and down over the curb. Pippin grabbed hold of Christopher to keep from being jolted out of his seat.

The car zigged and zagged and lurched down the road. Christopher had never actually driven the car before. At the corner light he skidded to a halt. The light turned green and the car lurched forward.

"Can't you drive this thing any better than that?" growled Pippin. "Here let me try."

"I'm getting it. I'm getting it. Leave me alone. Just keep your eyes on the map."

He put his foot on the accelerator and the car bounced down the street.

At the next traffic light they turned left, then left again. They were off the main roads without any street lights. Pippin squinted at his map. It was a dark night. He couldn't quite make out the turns.

"Wait a minute! Slow down. You missed a turn!"

Christopher slammed on the brakes and skidded to a halt.

He made a U-turn back to the corner. (Teddy bears, I'm afraid, have never heard of safety rules.) Ten minutes later Pippin was scratching his head trying to figure out where he had gone wrong.

"This can't be right. Piedmont Street shouldn't be here. They must have got the signs wrong."

"There's nothing wrong with the signs," growled Christopher. "You just don't know how to read a map."

"I do too. Pull over and you'll see. It's your driving that's crazy."

Christopher stopped the car, and the two bears huddled over the map. It was no easy task trying to read the street names by starlight.

"There it is. There's Piedmont," Christopher exclaimed. "Where have you been taking us? We're no where near where we should be."

He ran his paw over the map.

"If we turn around and take the second right, then the third left, then turn right again, we'll be all right."

He put his foot on the accelerator and spun the car around. The second right put them on a very bad road full of potholes.

"Hey! Watch where you're going. S^{low} d$_{own}$!" cried Pippin.

The car jolted into a pothole, bouncing the words right out of his mouth. He grabbed hold of Christopher. And just as he did, *he let go of the map!*

"Now you've done it!" cried Christopher. He screeched the car to a halt, and the two bears tumbled out. They raced after the map, but a gust of wind picked it up and blew it away. They ran as fast as their teddy bear legs could carry them, but it wasn't fast enough. The map blew up, over a fence, and away out of sight.

CHAPTER THREE
Lost

The two bears collapsed in a heap, gasping for breath.

"Now what do we do?" asked Pippin. We'll never find Maple Street, and we'll never find our way home."

"Nonsense. I said take the fourth right and then turn left, so that's what we'll do."

"I thought it was the second left."

"No, it wasn't. We've already done that. Just get in the car and don't argue."

So the two bears got in the car and very carefully counted four right turns and a left.

Christopher brought the car to a halt. "I don't understand. This should be Maple Street, and it's not. They must have got the signs wrong. Maybe if we go on a little further."

So they went a little further, but the road seemed to be taking them out into the country. That couldn't be right so they turned around again. They tried a left hand turn and then a right.

"It has to be around here somewhere," said Pippin. "Here wait, what did that sign say? Wasn't that Maple?"

"Where, what!" cried Christopher, turning around to look.

"**Hey!!!!** Watch where you're going! **Look out!!**"

The car bounced off the road and landed with a terrible grating noise in a ditch.

The bears sat dazed for a moment.

"Now what do we do?" asked Pippin a tiny little voice. He was beginning not to like this adventure at all.

Christopher didn't answer. He put the car in reverse and tried to back out. The wheels spun, and the engine made a high-pitched whining noise, but the car did not move.

Pippin got down and tried to push the car free. He grunted and groaned, but he couldn't budge it.

"Silly bears, it won't work." said a voice behind them.

Christopher and Pippin jumped. They spun around to find themselves face to face with a small smokey grey cat. She was sitting under the branches of an overgrown rose hedge. Her coat blended so well with the shadows they would never have seen her if she had not spoken.

CHAPTER FOUR
Feona

The cat stepped out of the shadows. "You'll never budge it," she said matter-of-factly.

"And what makes you so smart?" snarled Christopher. It wasn't polite, but nobody likes to be told what he already knows.

"Humph." said the cat. "I just know, that's all. I'm going home to my supper and a warm bed. You can come if you wish . . . . But if you want to stay here all night pushing at that car, it's all the same to me. You'll see I'm right."

She didn't wait for their answer, but turned around and strolled leisurely away.

Supper sounded very good, and a warm bed even better. The two bears picked themselves up and ran after her. But they needn't have hurried. Cats like to take their time. She took them under the rose hedge and across a large lawn lined with flower beds. She stopped often to sniff the wet grass. The bears could dimly see a house nestled under the shadows of two giant oak trees. It was a big old farmhouse, with a barn out in back.

"That's where I live," said the cat. "My name's Feona by the way. I'm glad you came. My family went away for the weekend, and I'm awfully bored. You can stay and keep me company."

She led them up to the back door. The bears were wondering how they were to get in, but Feona had a cat door so she could go in and out.

She pushed the flap open with her nose and disappeared into the house. Christopher went next. Halfway through he had the uncomfortable feeling he was going to get stuck.

He wiggled sideways while Pippin pushed from behind. It was quite a struggle, but suddenly he popped free onto the kitchen floor.

Pippin was next. Christopher grabbed hold of his paws and with a great heave-ho pulled him through.

Feona laughed at them "You are silly bears. How funny you look. You should see how dirty you are." The two bears looked sadly at one another. Their beautiful soft fur was covered with grime. They looked like very old, not very well loved bears.

"Never mind," said Feona. "I will lick you clean." And indeed, she did. The bears wiggled and giggled. They tried to sit still. Really, they did. But her tongue was so raspy, and it did tickle so.

"Really," said Feona, "you're worse than two kittens. Do sit still or we'll never get supper."

Finally, the job was done. The bears looked as bright and new as on the day they were made.

"Now what do bears eat, I wonder? Not cat food. Let me see what we have." She jumped up onto the counter. "Let's see, tea, coffee? Let me know when something sounds good. Cereal, crackers? There's some bread here. Jam. Honey . . ."

"Honey!" cried both bears together. "That's what bears like best."

"Then honey it is," said Feona. She rolled the jar over to the edge of the counter and knocked it off.

It landed bang on the floor, but it didn't break. They all jumped at the noise. But the house was empty. No one came running to see what was wrong. The bears struggled to get the lid off. It was all sticky and stuck to the jar. First Christopher tried, then Pippin, then Christopher tried again. Finally it came free, and the bears took turns sticking their paws in the jar.

"I don't know why I bothered cleaning you up. You're going to be twice as dirty with all that sticky honey on you." But the bears licked every bit off their coats, and then they licked the pot clean.

"I wonder what my family will think when they come home and find an empty honey jar, not to mention two fat teddy bears."

"Oh, but we can't stay," exclaimed Christopher. He'd forgotten all about Amber and the letter. He told Feona about their mission.

"Well, it seems to me you're stuck here," said Feona, "whether you like it or not. You've wrecked your car and you've lost your map. I don't know where Maple Street is. I suppose I could ask Ralph. He's a collie who lives across the street. But I doubt if he knows. He never goes anywhere."

"Well, Kenyon wouldn't just sit here," said Pippin. "He'd find something to do. If only we knew what."

"Then, why don't you call and ask him?" said Feona.

It was such a simple solution. It only shows how new to the world the bears were that they didn't think of it themselves. They knew the shop's telephone number. They had heard it given out often enough.

The kitchen phone hung up on the wall way out of reach for teddy bears. But the family room phone sat on a low table by the sofa. Christopher reached it by climbing first onto Pippin's back and then scrambling up onto the table.

The receiver was too big and heavy to hold. He knocked it off and let it lie on the table top. Bear paws aren't designed for dialing, but after several false starts, he managed it.

The shop bears were having a restless night, but they all jumped when the phone rang. Kenyon raced across the room to answer it. At four in the morning the only ones who could possibly be calling were Pippin and Christopher, in trouble.

He listened with a sinking feeling – no car, no map, no Amber, no way to get home, and, what was worse, no way of finding them. What on earth was he to do?

And then he thought, "I will send Bertram."

CHAPTER FIVE
Flight At Dawn

Bertram was a very special bear. He lived with the shop's owner, and he had his own aeroplane. He could fly out over Shuttle Hill until he spotted the car and the farmhouse, and then, and then . . . . Well, and then he could come back and tell them where the bears were and they'd figure out something.

He had Christopher describe the house in as much detail as he could. Then he hung up the phone and went himself to get Bertram.

Bertram lived across the street in the upstairs bedroom of a Victorian house. He shared the room with other bears and toys. Kenyon had been many times to visit.

The room was an old-fashioned children's nursery, except no children played there now. The bears had free run of all the toys, and it never occurred to them that they were anything but toys themselves.

Kenyon stole across the street. He knew where the key was kept, under the third flower pot on the right on the garage shelf. He let himself in and crept upstairs.

Bears can go very quietly when they want to. He wasn't afraid of waking anybody. He shut the nursery door softly behind him and went over to wake Bertram.

But Bertram was already awake. He was standing by his aeroplane in front of the window.

On clear nights such as this he liked to look at the stars and dream of flying. He was wearing his hat, goggles, and flying coat. A book about Charles Lindbergh lay half read on a table. That was the kind of adventure Bertram dreamed of.

He started when Kenyon came up behind him. But he was delighted to see him. "My dear chap, what on earth are doing here?"

Kenyon put his paw to his lips, and motioned him into a corner. "Shh, don't wake the others. I need your help."

In half whispered tones he told Bertram all about the evening's adventure.

"Can you find them? I thought if you could spot the house from your plane, you could tell us how to find them, and then, well . . . ."

"Yes . . . . and then?"

"Well, then we'll rescue them, but first we have to know where they are." Bertram didn't argue. Any excuse to fly his plane was more than welcome.

Kenyon opened the window for him. It was just wide enough for the wings to fit through. Bertram climbed into the cockpit, threw his scarf over his shoulder, and signalled Kenyon with a paws up – all systems go!

The engine roared (well, actually sputtered) to life. It wobbled once, twice around the bedroom floor to pick up speed, then flew out the window.

Kenyon watched the tiny craft rock back and forth until a wind caught it and carried it up over the trees and away out of sight.

The sky was just beginning to lighten as Bertram started out. A rosy glow showed along the horizon. In half an hour it would be light. He let his plane fly just above the treetops. From the ground what you saw were houses and green lawns. But from the air you saw trees. It was hard to believe that beneath him were hundreds and hundreds of houses. The trees of the suburbs blended with the trees of the country in a beautiful rolling sea of green.

He flew back and forth across the main road. He had no idea what route the bears had taken, but this let him see the entire town. The newer sections looked ugly from the air. The houses were big square boxes without any green trees to hide them. Bertram shied away from these. The house he wanted was old with gingerbread work around the front porch. He concentrated most of his efforts to the left of the main road. That was where the older houses seemed to be. He flew up higher to scout the area and saw a touch of silver glistening in the early morning light. Flying over it, he saw a pond with a barn near it, and a white farmhouse. In front of the house were rows of neatly kept flower beds and a rose hedge bordering the road. He even caught a glimpse of a green car lying in the ditch. He had no doubts. This was the house.

But now the problem was how to get back to the shop, and how to tell the other bears how to get to it. He flew up higher so he could see the whole town laid out beneath him.

"Those silly bears," Bertram laughed to himself. "I bet they drove in circles all night to get here." The house lay on a country road on the outskirts of town, but two stop signs and a right hand turn brought him back to the same road the shop was on.

He flew low again, mapping out a route for the bears. Below him the town was just beginning to wake up. As yet no people were abroad. It was Sunday morning and everyone was sleeping in. But as he swung round for one more pass over the area, the silence was broken by the barking of very fierce looking dog.

Bertram was glad he was in his plane, and the dog safely behind a fence. He thought of Amber trapped in a house by just such a dog. And then he thought again.

"By jove, yes!" He flew close to the ground along the street, dangerously so as the wind rocked his plane, but he had seen enough. The sign post at the corner said "Maple Street!"

Once more he flew up to get his bearings. And then he followed the roads home. He landed very neatly on the sidewalk just in front of the shop.

CHAPTER SIX
An Unexpected Friend

Kenyon was waiting for Bertram's return. Together they wheeled the plane into the shop. The other bears cheered him as he came in. Bertram felt quite embarrassed. He hadn't done that much.

"Did you find them? Did you find them?" they all shouted at once.

"Yes, and I did better than that. I found Maple Street." He told them all about his flight and what he had seen.

"We must form an expetition," said a little bear who liked to use big words even when he really didn't know them.

"A what?" laughed Kenyon.

"An expetition!" Ever since he'd been the drummer in the bear's Memorial Day parade, he'd wanted to lead a march down main street.

"I hardly think that will get you anywhere,"said Bertram, "except into more trouble. People – especially grown-up people – don't see very much, but they'd have to notice a whole band of teddy bears marching up the street. Besides, it would take you a month of Sundays to get there. It's miles and miles.

"But what else can we do?" said another bear.

"Yes indeed," said Kenyon, "we've lost the car, and your plane isn't big enough for two bears, let alone three or four."

"Excuse me," said a rusty voice from the front of the room. "I can help."

The bears jumped. They thought they were alone in the shop. The voice had come from the window, but nobody was there. In fact all that was in the window were a few chairs and a big metal horse the bears liked to sit on.

But that was what, or rather *who*, was talking. There could be no doubt about it. He talked very slowly. The hinge at his jaw was almost rusted shut. It made his voice very gravelly.

He stepped stiff legged from the window. "I could help," he said again. "I'm faster'n teddy bear legs."

The teddy bears had never seen him move so much as an inch. They were as surprised as you or I would be to see him come alive and walk across the floor.

Chester, a big honey colored bear who rode him the most went up to him. "Why didn't you let me know you were real?"

"I didn't have nothin' to say."

"Do you have a name?"

"Hector. Least ways, that's what they used to call me, before they growed up and forgot all about me." A tear rolled down his metal face.

"Now, now, none of that," said Chester. "What do you think, Kenyon? I could ride him, and we could at least get Pippin and Christopher back."

"Well." said Kenyon hesitating for a moment. "It does seem the only thing to do. Only do be careful. We can't be rescuing you, too."

Bertram went over the way to the farmhouse three or four times, and then the way to Maple Street.

"Don't worry," said Chester. "I'll remember." Then he put on his cowboy hat, tightened the kerchief around his neck and got on Hector.

The bears cheered them on their way. Chester wished they could have
reared up and gone galloping off like the Lone Ranger. And he really
wished he had a mask.

"Who was that masked bear?" he said to himself.

"Eh, what?" said Hector.

"Nothing, er nothing at all," stammered Chester.

Hector had only two gaits, a slow walk, and a stiff legged gallop. The
walk wasn't hard to sit, but the gallop was horrendous. Chester
grabbed hold of Hector's mane and prayed that he wouldn't
fall off. He was feeling less and less like the Lone Ranger as
he bounced up and down on Hector's hard metal back. His
hooves made an awful racket on the road. But it was early
still, not even six o'clock on a Sunday morning and nobody
seemed to notice.

Bertram had given good directions, the kind with lots of landmarks.
Everything was just as he described, the school where they made their first
turn, the little shopping plaza and the cemetery. The road brought them
into the country. Houses yielded to trees, and before they knew it, they
were looking across a dense rose hedge to the farmhouse.

They found the green car easily enough and followed Feona's path
under the roses. Chester had to get down off Hector and crawl
through. He was taller than the other bears. The prickers
snagged his fur, but they couldn't do anything
to Hector's metal back. He walked through the
briars as though they weren't even there.

They went up to the back porch
and Chester poked his head through
Feona's cat door. That was as far as
he could go. He was too big
to get the rest of himself in.

"Pippin! Christopher!"
he called, but the house
was silent. He saw the
empty honey jar lying on
the kitchen floor, but no
bears.

"It would be
just like those
two to call for help
and then go off
on a wild goose
chase."

"They could just
be sleeping." Hector
said. "Stand on my
back. You ought'a
be able to see in
the windows."

So that's what they did. At
each of the ground floor windows Chester
stood up on tiptoe balanced across the saddle. He could just see over the
window ledge into each room. The front windows were hard because the
bushes rubbed right up against the house. He had to hold onto the ledge
with one paw and push branches away with the other.

The living room and dining room were empty, as was the downstairs study, but when he peered into the family room he saw three sleeping figures curled up together on the couch.

With his teddy bear paws, Chester made a BANG! BANG! BANG! on the window. Feona started from her sleep. She was off the couch and halfway out the door before you could say "boo". Chester banged on the glass again, but bears are heavy sleepers and they didn't stir.

Feona felt braver now that she was awake. She crept back into the room and eyed the window.

"Why, it's another bear!" she exclaimed, and suddenly she felt much braver. She jumped up onto the window ledge, knocking over a geranium pot in the process. It crashed to the floor spilling dirt all over the carpet. Feona ignored it. It was a silly place for a plant to be, especially when she wanted to sit on the ledge herself.

"Wake them up," Chester yelled, banging again on the glass.

"What?"

"Wake them up and come out."

"I can't hear you."

Chester mustered all of the breath he had and tried again. But he needn't have bothered. The crash from the pot had done the trick. Both bears sat up, rubbing the sleep from their eyes.

"Who's Feona talking to?"

"I can't believe it! Why, that's Chester!"

They tumbled off the couch and ran to the window. After much gesturing and shouting, Chester got them to understand that he couldn't get in and they were to come out.

CHAPTER SEVEN
To The Rescue

The two bears were just a little bit bigger after eating all that honey. They got stuck trying to squeeze through the cat door. Chester grabbed each one by the paws and pulled.

"You're killing me!" growled Christopher. He had eaten the most and was the fattest.

Chester ignored him and just tugged harder – Pop! – he came free, and they both went tumbling backwards down the steps.

"How did you find us? Can we get back? Did anyone else come?"

"Hey, one question at a time. I didn't find you. Bertram did, in his aeroplane. You two really have made a mess of things. I saw the car. Is it totally wrecked?"

"I don't know," said Pippin. "We couldn't get it out of the ditch."

"Well, with three of us and Hector we ought at least to be able to do that."

Feona led them back to the ditch and jumped up on the hood of the car.

"I'll direct," she declared, and so she did. But it didn't take much direction, just a lot of pushing and shoving, to get the car free.

"Well," said Christopher doubtfully. "It looks all right." He started up the engine and it sputtered into life. "It sounds all right."

He put his foot on the accelerator and the car lurched sideways, nearly knocking over the other bears. "Hey, watch out!" growled Chester.

Christopher only just missed sending the car back into the ditch.

"There, er, there's something wrong with the steering."

"I'll say," said Chester. "Well, so much for using the car. We can't all ride on Hector, so you two will just have to walk. I don't think it's far."

"What isn't far?" asked Pippin.

"Maple Street, of course, or had you forgotten what you came for?"

"Of course we hadn't, but we can't go to Maple Street. We don't know where it is."

"But I do," said Chester, and he told them all about Bertram and his flight.

Christopher and Pippin grumbled at having to walk, but Chester shut them up.

"You wrecked the car, don't forget." he said. So they hid it back under the rose hedge, and the five of them started out. Chester led the way on Hector. Pippin and Christopher came next, and Feona brought up the rear.

Maple Street wasn't really very far, only a couple of blocks, but that can be a very long way for short teddy bear legs. They walked on the sidewalk and tried to keep out of sight. The traffic was picking up, but they needn't have worried. People, especially grown-up people, only see what they expect to see. One little girl waved to them and tried to get her parents to stop, but they only told her to stop telling such stories.

So the bears found Maple Street and the house with the high fence around it to keep in the dog. He let out a terrible baying as soon as he saw them, and came bounding up to the fence.

Feona shot back under a bush. She liked dogs, nice shaggy, bushy tailed dogs who came up to her with a wag and a grin. This kind of angry, baying, barking dog she wanted no part of.

The bears shrank back, too. They wanted to help – really they did – but now that they saw the dog and the house it all looked so hopeless.

Chester tried the diplomat's way.

"My dear sir," he began, but the dog snarled at him and lunged at the fence.

Just then the front door opened and the family came out, Mother, Father, a grubby-faced little girl, and the boy – the boy who had torn holes in Amber's fur and nearly drowned him in the bathtub.

"I can see him doing it," said Pippin. "He's got the look."

"I'll bet he whines for candy when he's out shopping," said Christopher.

"I don't like him," said Chester, "and no matter what it takes we are going to rescue Amber."

The others agreed. Just how, they would work out later. Right now their chief concern was not being seen. The bears dove down into the weeds, and Hector tried to look invisible behind a fence post.

"What's that fool dog barking at?" growled the father. "Hey, Roman, stop that! Come here. Get over here."

The dog ignored him. He snarled at the bears and dug at the bottom of the fence. The little boy picked up a stone and threw it at him.

"Hey, don't do that!" shouted his father, grabbing him by the shoulder and giving him a good shake. "Get in the car, all of you. He'll stop barking as soon as we leave."

He pushed his son towards the car. As soon as it had pulled out of the drive and disappeared down the road, the bears came out of hiding.

CHAPTER EIGHT
Escape!

"I'll get you," snarled the dog. "Come near and I'll eat you!"

Chester tried to ignore him. He saw a maple tree leaning up against the house, and that gave him an idea.

"If we could get to that tree," he said, "we could climb up to that window. You see the one? It's open. We could just about reach it from that branch."

"Yes," said Pippin, "but first you have to get to the tree. How are you going to do that?"

"Hmmm, well, . . . er. . . . He can't get all of us, not if we all run across at once. Someone's bound to make it."

"Now that's a jolly thought," began Pippin, but Feona interrupted him.

"I'll draw him away. He'll chase me and that'll give you time to get to the tree."

She sounded very brave, but inside she was shaking like a leaf.

"And I'll take you across," said Hector.

Christopher started to argue, but Chester interrupted him. "It's a good plan. In fact, it's the only plan. Feona, you are a truly great friend."

"Never mind that," said Feona, getting embarrassed. "Just be ready." She ran down the fence line, but the dog didn't follow.

"Here goes everything," said Feona. She jumped up onto a fence post and down into the yard. The dog spun round and gave chase. Feona dashed for the house. She'd spotted a gap under the foundation. She raced for that, with the dog right on her heels.

"I'll get you! I'll get you!" he snarled, but Feona ducked down the hole. It led nowhere, it was just a damp gap in the foundation stones. The dog pressed his jaws through, snapping at air, and digging with his paws. Feona pressed back against the wall. Her heart was thump, thumping. He'd get her! The hole was getting bigger with his frantic digging.

And then suddenly he was gone, chasing after Hector who was making a mad dash for the tree. Chester clung to his neck and prayed he wouldn't fall off. Hector had taken a running start and jumped the fence. Chester hadn't known what to do, but he held on tightly and closed his eyes. The dog was coming up behind them, snarling and barking.

"Hurry Hector! *Hurry!*" Chester shouted in his ear.

Hector gave what felt like a big buck and kicked out with his hind legs. The dog reeled backwards head over heels.

That gave them a moment's edge, enough to reach the tree and for Chester to scramble up into its lower branches. The dog was right back again, snapping at Hector's heels. But he couldn't hurt his hard metal legs and Chester was up out of reach. Teddy Bears aren't very good at running, but they are very good at climbing trees. In a moment Chester was inching his was along the top branches that brushed against the house.

He could see into an upstairs bedroom. It was a boy's room. The walls were lined with posters, big ugly posters of space invaders and rock stars. The floor was littered with clothes and toys, and, off in one corner, a teddy bear! Chester almost didn't recognize him.

He slumped limply against the dresser. He was missing an ear, and the stuffing was poking out of his paws. But worse yet, the boy had taken scissors and cut off great patches of his fur. It made him look more like a space monster than a teddy bear, but that was what the boy wanted.

Chester tapped on the glass. "Amber! Amber! Wake up. We've come for you." But the bear didn't hear.

Chester lowered himself down from the branch to the window ledge. Below him the dog was barking and snapping at Hector. He forced himself not to look down or to think what would happen if he fell.

The window was open just wide enough for him to squeeze through. He fell – Plop – onto the floor.

"Amber, Amber, wake up!" He shook him hard, but Amber did not move.

Teddy bears who are not loved slowly start to lose themselves. It becomes harder and harder for them to be roused, until eventually all the shouting, and shaking, and loving in the world will not bring them to life again. Amber was gradually drifting off. His mind was getting fuzzy, and he seldom stirred. He stared at Chester without understanding.

"Come on Amber, we haven't much time."

"What? Why are you here? You won't like it here."

"I know I won't. I've come to rescue you. Remember your letter?"

"My letter? . . . . My letter!" and a look of understanding came into his eyes. "My letter. Kenyon did get it!" Then he stopped. He was listening to the terrible barking of the dog. "But you're trapped, too. How can we get out with that dog down below?"

"I got in, we can get out," declared Chester. He tried to sound as though it would be the easiest thing in the world to do.

He pulled Amber to his feet. Their first problem was how to get up onto the window. But that was easily solved. The boy never put anything away. All his clothes were heaped in piles about the floor. The two bears dragged them over to the window until they had built up a huge mound. They used it just like a set of stairs to climb up and sit comfortably on the window ledge. Amber looked down at the dog, and across to the tree branch. From this angle it looked very far away.

"Ooh, I can't do it. I can't! I'll fall!"

"No, you won't. You'll see," said Chester. He leaned way out of the window and grabbed hold of the tree branch. It took all his strength to pull it closer. "Hurry!" he gasped. "I can't hold it long."

Amber didn't argue. He scrambled up onto the branch. Then Chester jumped off of the window ledge and hung for a moment with his feet dangling in mid-air.

The branch bounced wildly up and down. Amber felt seasick, but he grabbed hold of Chester's paws to help keep him from falling.

"Hang on!" Amber cried. "*Please*, don't let go."

Chester prayed he wouldn't. He kicked up with his feet, trying to swing them up over the branch. He tried three times before he finally succeeded. Amber pulled him up the rest of the way, then they scrambled back towards the trunk.

Feona had been watching for them. As soon as they were half way down the tree, she shot out of her hiding place. She called to the dog who was still worrying at Hector's heels. He reeled round and charged after her. Feona flew across the yard and up over the fence. There she turned, arched her back and hissed at the dog. But he could only growl and bark stupidly along the fence line.

That's what the two bears were waiting for. They scurried down the last few branches of the tree, and dropped onto Hector's back.

The dog saw them and tore after them. Hector raced for the fence with the bears hanging on for dear life. He jumped it with the dog snapping at his heels. Amber and Chester tumbled off at the landing, but it didn't matter – not on this side of the fence – and teddy bears do not have bones to break.

They looked back. The dog was snarling more viciously than ever, leaping high at the top of the fence.

"Come on!" shouted Feona. "*RUN!*" She didn't wait for the bears. She shot off for home, and they followed as fast as their teddy bear legs could take them.

CHAPTER NINE
A Parting Of Friends

When they could run no further and the dog's barking was only a distant grumble, they all collapsed in a heap. Feona came over and licked Amber's face to make him feel better.

They rested for a time under a bush, then they got up and began the long march back to Feona's house.

It was dusk when they arrived. They pulled the car out of its hiding place. Christopher jiggled the steering wheel, but it was well and truly jammed.

Hector pressed his nose against the cold metal hood. "If we was to have a rope, I could pull it," he said.

"Pull it! All that way?" exclaimed Chester.

"Aye. I used to be a cart horse, before I was a riding horse. As far as I can see, a car's just a funny looking cart."

"Well . . ." said Chester.

"I don't see any other way," said Christopher. "Feona you wouldn't happen to know where we could find a rope, would you?"

"Yes, well . . . there's rope in the old barn, tons of it. But if I show you, you'll leave."

"We should have to leave anyway. We don't belong here. We belong at the shop where people can adopt us."

Feona twitched her tail. Then without saying a word, she led them to the barn.

It stood off by itself at the back of the house. The doors were shut tight, but Feona knew all the secret ways in. They found the rope buried under a pile of old newspapers. The papers spilled all over the floor when they pulled it out.

"My family is in for some surprises," laughed Feona, regaining her spirits. "First the honey pot and now this. "They're always saying the house is haunted. Now they'll really believe it."

The rope was just the right length for pulling the car. Pippin got the job of crawling underneath it to tie the rope to the front axle. They tied the other end round Hector. He pulled and the others all pushed. But once the car got moving it rolled very easily along the road.

It was now well after dark and the streets were quiet. Chester climbed onto Hector's back and Pippin, Amber, and Christopher rode in the car.

Feona started out with them, but when they got to the end of her road, she stopped.

Good-byes can be very sad and awkward, especially when there are so many thank yous to be said. Feona didn't want to hear any of it.

A car pulled into the road just as they were all fumbling for the right words. Feona interrupted them all. "That's my family. They're home! I must go, or they'll miss me." And she disappeared like a shot into the shadows.

"It must be nice to have a family," sighed Pippin.

"No, it isn't," said Amber, "believe me!"

The trek home was a long one. The bears were all nodding with sleep when Hector finally reached the shop.

Chester tumbled off and banged on the window to rouse the bears. A great cheering went up from inside, and in a moment the front door was open, and they were being given a hero's welcome home.

CHAPTER TEN
A Gift Of Love

Monday morning when the shop opened for business, all the bears were back in their proper places. The car had been scrubbed clean, and the steering wheel repaired. Hector had some new scratches from the dog, but the owners didn't seem to notice. What they did notice was a very sad looking bear propped up by the desk. His stuffing was falling out, an ear was missing, and his fur was stained and in places sheared off.

"Where on earth did he come from?" they wondered. The bears all knew. They winked at one another. It was hard work not to laugh, but they never did tell.

The shop owners sent Amber off to Jane Kenyon for repairs. Mrs. Kenyon had made all of the teddy bears, even Kenyon, which was how he got his name. She gave Amber a new ear, and new pads, and cleaned the stains off his front. But she couldn't do anything for the great bald patches on his stomach. So she made him a wonderful sailor suit that hid them all.

Amber loved his fine new outfit. And Mrs. Kenyon was so kind that he almost forgot about the horrid little boy and his dog. He told Mrs. Kenyon about him. Most grown-ups don't listen to bears, but Mrs. Kenyon did, and she knew exactly the cure Amber needed.

The next day she invited a little neighbor girl in. Her name was Ann, and she had always wanted a teddy bear.

When she saw Amber she couldn't resist. She had to pick him up and love him. Mrs. Kenyon looked at Amber, and Amber smiled back.

"Ann dear, this bear has had a very hard time. He has been very badly abused. Do you think you could take him home and love him very much, so he will feel better?"

Ann's eyes lit up. "Do you mean it? Oh, yes!" And she gave Amber a great big bear hug.

And so, Amber went home with Ann and learned what it really meant to have a family. He always had a smile on his face, and in his teddy bear heart he knew what it was to love.

AFTERWORD

Kenyon came to visit this morning. He told me the oddest thing has happened. Christopher and Pippin have a new home. A lady came into the shop and took them *both* away. Kenyon got a letter from them yesterday, and do you know where they are? Why, with Feona. It was her family who adopted them! I suppose it could just be coincidence, but I think it's magic. Kenyon thinks so, too.

Chester said he doesn't want to be adopted. He wants to stay in the shop and keep Hector company. I think Kenyon is pleased about that. He told me another story. It's called *Edgrr Who Would Be Real*. And no, I won't tell it to you now. You have to wait.

The beary end.

We wish to thank everyone who helped with our story: Mrs. K. for making the bears, and Mrs. K for giving them a home; Victor for speeding things up, and Mr. K. for intoducing us to him; Mr. K. for helping around the joints; Emil and Carol Kuhl for sharing their toys with the bears; Wendy Birkemeier for the chapters; Betsy Ellsworth for her patience and good suggestions (the bears promise that next time they'll sit still for the camera); the staff at the State University at Albany who helped with the typesetting and layout; and, of course, the bears themselves.